When Shepherds Bleed

A Study Guide for Wounded Pastors

T.D. Jakes
Stanley Miller

When Shepherds Bleed

A Study Guide for Wounded Pastors

by T.D. Jakes and Stanley Miller

Printed in the United States of America

When Shepherds Bleed - Study Guide
ISBN 1-56229-446-6

Pneuma Life Publishing
4451 Parliament Place
Lanham, MD 20706 U.S.A.
(301) 577-4052
(301) 577-4935 Fax
(800) 727-3218

http://www.pneumalife.com

Table of Contents

Chapter   Page

Preface

Many of God's shepherds are wounded.

More serious, however, is the fact that even more are bleeding. When shepherds bleed, they can die; if they die, then an entire flock may suffer.

In the pages that follow, we will examine your wounds and allow them to bleed long enough to remove any remaining bitterness or malice that could hinder the process of healing.

As you complete this study, I pray that your bleeding will stop and your wounds will be healed. May God, by His Spirit, infuse and transfuse you with new life to restore you to your full potential.

To God Be All The Glory for the things He will do!

The Eyes of a Lamb

If you need a good boxing trainer, you don't want someone who has been sitting on the sidelines. No, you look for a person who has been on the inside of the ring. As a former boxer, he knows what it means to be under subjection to a trainer. He knows what it feels like to be knocked down and to get back up. He has also learned from experience how to guard the vital areas.

The best football coach is the guy who can relate to what happens on the field. If he has been a player himself, he knows how it feels to be hurt yet tape up the wounds on game day and help the team win.

Like the boxing trainer or the football coach, a shepherd must understand what it means to be a sheep. The best pastors are able to relate to their flock because they have seen the pasture through the eyes of a lamb.

As we near the end of this dispensation of grace, God is going to be asking a lot of His leaders. The greatest demand to be placed upon you, as a pastor, will be learning how to teach your people to meet the challenges of life. Perhaps the best way to do this is for you to become who they are, for a season, so you can relate to what they are feeling.

In other words, you—as God's shepherd—need to develop the eyes of a lamb.

Developing a Shepherd's Heart

Before God allowed Moses, the adopted son of Pharaoh's daughter, to lead His people out of Egypt, God sent Moses to the backside of a desert for forty years. These were not years without purpose.

While Moses tended to the flock of his father-in-law, Jethro, he learned to look through the eyes of a lamb (Exodus 3:1-15).

Moses also learned that I AM, the great Shepherd, was the source of sustenance for the flock (Exodus 3:1,13).

God used these years of preparation to develop in Moses what he could only learn by being a shepherd.

The same was true of King David.

God's shepherds have shepherds' hearts.

When God needed a king to replace Saul, God chose David — the one no one else would have chosen.

Again, Jesse made seven of his sons to pass before Samuel. And Samuel said unto Jesse, The Lord hath not chosen these. And Samuel said unto Jesse, Are here all thy children? And he said, There remaineth yet the youngest, and, behold, he keepeth the sheep. And Samuel said unto Jesse, Send and fetch him: for we will not sit down till he come hither. And he sent, and brought him in. Now he was ruddy, and withal of a beautiful countenance, and goodly to look to. And the Lord said, Arise, anoint him: for this is he. Then Samuel took the horn of oil, and anointed him in the midst of his brethren: and the Spirit of the Lord came upon David from that day forward. So Samuel rose up, and went to Ramah. 1 Samuel 16:10-13

When Jesse's sons were asked to candidate for king, David was not invited. As the youngest, he was considered too immature for the job. In spite of the fact that David was an outcast in many ways, he had something special going for him. David had a shepherd's heart, and God knew it.

David had proven himself in the way he cared for the sheep. Many times he had wiped blood from wounds that a lamb had suffered through a fall or from the attack of a lion.

> *And David said unto Saul, Thy servant kept his father's sheep, and there came a lion, and a bear, and took a lamb out of the flock: And I went out after him, and smote him, and delivered it out of his mouth: and when he arose against me, I caught him by his beard, and smote him, and slew him. Thy servant slew both the lion and the bear: and this uncircumcised Philistine shall be as one of them, seeing he hath defied the armies of the living God. David said moreover, The Lord that delivered me out of the paw of the lion, and out of the paw of the bear, he will deliver me out of the hand of this Philistine. And Saul said unto David, Go, and the Lord be with thee.*
> *Samuel 17:34-37* ·

David understood the fears that sheep have. He knew they are afraid of rushing water. If a lamb falls in a stream of water, the lining of their wool becomes saturated with water, and the lamb drowns.

When waters opposed the sheep and caused them to fear, David took rocks and dammed up the waters so that he could then lead them beside the stilled waters.

> *He maketh me to lie down in green pastures: he leadeth me beside the still waters. Psalm 23:2*

David knew when to feed his sheep. When the flock became weary, David would find a good grazing spot and make them lie down in green pastures to find rest for the journey.

Do you as a pastor know and understand your flock? Do you recognize and allay their fears? Do you know how to feed them with God's Word and when to encourage them in their weariness?

The heart of God is a heart for people.

The Frail Side of Leadership

The lessons David learned as a shepherd carried over into his character as a person. In fact, David had several characteristics that made him stand out from the other men of his day.

> *And when he had removed him, he raised up unto them David to be their king; to whom also he gave testimony, and said, I have found David the son of Jesse, a man after mine own heart, which shall fulfil all my will. Of this man's seed hath God according to his promise raised unto Israel a Saviour, Jesus. Acts 13:22-23*

From the apostle Paul's description of David we learn three things:

1. David was a man after God's own heart. In other words, he had a heart for people.

2. David was a man who would fulfill God's will. He had a heart of obedience.

3. David was a man of destiny from whose seed Israel's Savior would come.

David became King, but he never lost his identity with the lamb. Although it was not the sovereign will of God for David to fall into sin with Bathsheba, through his fall we can relate to the forgiveness, restoration, and mercy of God.

We, as Christian leaders and pastors, are God's anointed shepherds, but we also have the frailties of a lamb. We have power to slay the Goliaths who defy the armies of God and the potential to be enticed by the Bathsheba's of our day.

These two identities allow us to have a unique relationship with God and at the same time help us to relate to the sheep. The frail side of pastors is seldom seen, but it is as much a reality as the side of us that rises to leadership. It is called humanity.

Though David fell and was judged by God, God took what the devil intended for evil and brought good out of it. The seed of David produced another shepherd who would look through the eyes of a lamb. David had within his loins a shepherd — Solomon.

> *And David comforted Bathsheba his wife, and went in unto her, and lay with her: and she bare a son, and he called his name Solomon: and the Lord loved him.*
> *2 Samuel 12:24*

> *Through the seed of Solomon came a lineage that would bring forth the Great Shepherd, the Savior Jesus*
> *Matthew 1:6-23.*

Within your soul is a seed that God intends to use to produce shepherds who will see through the eyes of a lamb, walk as a lamb, and experience life as a lamb. God plans to take the lambs you have shepherded and produce from them, shepherds — even as He promised to do through the seed of David.

Jesus the Lamb; Christ the Shepherd

Jesus Christ the same yesterday, and today, and for ever.
Hebrews 13:8

In this verse, there is both "Jesus" and "Christ." Jesus was His earthly name, and Christ speaks of His deity and divinity.

Jesus, whom John the Baptist referred to as "the Lamb of God," knows the needs of a lamb (John 1:29). Yet as Christ, He is the Chief Shepherd who can attend to those needs. His ministry of shepherdhood was preceded by His walking as a Lamb.

As a Lamb, Jesus Christ could relate to humanity; as a Shepherd, He was greatly moved with compassion (Matthew 9:36).

The nursery rhyme, "Mary Had a Little Lamb," reminds us of a remarkable truth. Mary really did have a Little Lamb: Jesus the Spotless Lamb of God.

To help us understand how weary a lamb can become, Jesus endured a wilderness of temptation and was tempted in all points as we are (Matthew 4:1-10).

> *Seeing then that we have a great high priest, that is passed into the heavens, Jesus the Son of God, let us hold fast our profession. For we have not an high priest which cannot be touched with the feeling of our infirmities; but was in all points tempted like as we are, yet without sin. Let us therefore come boldly unto the throne of grace, that we may obtain mercy, and find grace to help in time of need.*
> *Hebrews 4:14-16*

He walked through storms to see how helpless a lamb can be and to also feel the fear and despair.

He saw the hunger and thirst of a wandering soul who longed to come home to the outstretched arms of a loving Father. Jesus called the lamb a prodigal, but He understood the young man's dilemma, seeing it through the eyes of a lamb (Luke 15:3-24).

The most humbling and heartbreaking cries that have ever echoed on this earth were the cries of the Lamb of God on a small, lonely hill called Mt. Calvary—Golgotha—the place of the skull.

Have you ever heard the innocent, defenseless bleating of a helpless lamb? The sound tears at the heart.

Jesus cried out on Calvary's mountain that day, causing the earth to convulse with sorrow.

> *And about the ninth hour Jesus cried with a loud voice, saying, Eli, Eli, lama sabachthani? that is to say, My God, my God, why hast thou forsaken me?*
> *Matthew 27:46*

His cries from the cross still echo in the souls of Christians who commit themselves to the ultimate will of God by dying to their flesh as a lamb.

The Best Shepherds

God is calling a few good men and women to feed his flock and to do it faithfully. God did not call us to be judges, prosecutors, or accusers, but rather He called us to be shepherds. I am convinced that the best shepherds are those who look through the eyes of a lamb.

Ministry is sometimes so demanding that many pastors come to the place where they wonder, "Will I make it? Can I possibly go another step?"

You may be questioning where you are in your ministry and why you face seemingly endless challenges. Keep in mind that you cannot understand how it feels to be poor if you have always been rich. You can never know what it means to have to make it if you have always had it made.

Whatever you are going through in your life will make you a better pastor—and a more sympathetic person. God wants you to develop a shepherd's heart, and He is doing that by allowing you to see through the eyes of a lamb.

Once you have been on the playing field and inside the boxing ring, you are able to relate to the struggles of those trying to win the prize. If you have experienced the trials and temptations of life, it makes you more understanding and not nearly as judgmental.

God allowed Jesus to become a Shepherd of sheep so He could relate as a Shepherd of souls. Why would He expect anything less of us?

God allowed Jesus to become a Shepherd of sheep so He could relate as a Shepherd of souls.

Questions

1. What areas in Moses' life do you feel God was dealing with during the forty years Moses was on the backside of the desert?_____

_____

_____

_____

2. Using Psalm 23, list characteristics (other than the three mentioned) of a shepherd's heart._____

_____

_____

_____

_____

_____

_____

3. Why did God say David was "a man after mine own heart"?_____

_____

_____

_____

4. What characteristics make you stand out from the men or women of your day? List at least three._____

_____

_____

_____

_____

5. Describe one of your frailties as a lamb, and tell how God is using it to help you relate to others struggling with the same weakness.

_____

_____

_____

_____

_____

6. How is God using you to produce other shepherds?_____

_____

_____

_____

_____

_____

7. Explain how Jesus, as the Lamb of God, is able to relate to our struggles as human beings._____

_____

_____

_____

_____

8. How is God allowing you to develop a shepherd's heart?_____

_____

_____

_____

_____

9. Why is it so important for a pastor to be familiar with the struggles faced by his flock?_____

_____

_____

_____

_____

_____

10. In what ways can you use your past failures to help your congregation?_____

_____

_____

_____

_____

11. In your own words, use Psalm 51 to form a five point outline to aid a fallen pastor.

     I.   _____

          A. _____

          B. _____

     II.   _____

          A. _____

          B._____

III. _____

    A. _____

    B. _____

IV. _____

    A. _____

    B. _____

V. _____

    A. _____

    B. _____

12. Explain how God is working in your life to produce the eyes of a lamb._____

_____

_____

_____

_____

Notes

Notes

Notes

When Shepherds Cry Out

Throughout Scripture every person who was used by God suffered traumatic, difficult, and hurtful events in his or her life. In fact, a careful study in the Word reveals that God never chose to use anyone greatly whom He did not first choose to allow to be hurt deeply.

Let's examine some of the great shepherds of God's flock whose bleeding has significance for us today.

The Shepherd's Cry

Adam's son, Abel, was a shepherd. From his murder, the first recorded in the Bible, we learn some key principles. After Cain killed his brother Abel, the Lord said, ". . . the voice of thy brother's blood crieth unto me from the ground" (Genesis 4:10).

To understand what this verse really means, we need to examine it more closely. The Hebrew word for "voice" is *qol-kole*, which means a bleating, crackling sound; a proclamation; a significant definite sound with a thundering effect.

In this verse, the word "blood" means to die, to shed drops of blood, to cease to be, to be silent, or to be dormant.

"Crieth" means to shriek with a shrill voice, to awaken, to call together an assembly by means of its lamenting effect.

Adam, the Hebrew word for "ground," relates to the original creation of man and means soil, or earthy; to show redness; to be rosy or flush as blood.

Genesis 4:10 says the voice of Abel's blood cried out from the ground. Why? Because the blood, which caused him to live and to function, had been transfused into Abel by God–through the seed of Adam. Abel's blood cried out as it saw itself going back to its original form. Since the Bible says the life of the flesh is in the blood, it would be safe to say that the very essence of Abel's life, the very fiber of his being, was voicing one last gasp.

Using the fuller meanings of the words of Genesis 4:10, we can paraphrase the cry that Abel's blood made to God: "The very life within me, my purpose, my goals, my dreams, everything You ever said I was or could be, with a thundering, lamenting cry, shakes beyond the grave. I have put back into the earth that which, before it touched me, was only a form without any real purpose or worth. What you placed in me has been murdered. My real life, my blood, which makes me who I am and gives me the ability to become who you want me to be, cries out, 'Help me. I am a bleeding and dying shepherd. My cry comes up to You. You can change it and make it right.'" Is that your cry today? If so, you are not alone.

Bleeding Shepherds of the Old Testament

Three of the greatest men in the Old Testament were shepherds who reached the full potential of God's purpose in their lives because of the suffering and hurts they experienced.

Moses

As the infant Moses floated down the river in an ark of bulrushes, he cried. Moses' usefulness to God began when he was drawn out of the water by the servants of Pharaoh's daughter. In fact, the name, Moses, means "to draw out."

Later, during Moses' stay on the backside of a desert, God let him see through the eyes of a lamb. Before Moses could be trusted to lead God's people out of Egypt, Moses had to become intimately attached to a common flock of sheep.

That drawing out required that Moses bleed until, finally, God heard his cries and met him in a divine way. It took 40 years, but God drew the character of a shepherd out of the life of Moses.

David

The shepherd David's bleeding was fourfold:
1. He bled while protecting his sheep from the enemies that would have hurt them (I Samuel 17:34-36).
2. He bled by the hands of his own family members; he was not even invited to the coronation of a king over Israel. His heart, no doubt, bled from rejection (I Samuel 16:8-13).
3. His hands and feet bled from leading and shepherding his sheep. Every drop of blood and every scar was a lesson, a day in school, as God groomed David for greatness (Psalm 23).
4. If we read 2 Samuel 11 along with Psalm 51, we see a shepherd who bled because of adultery, lying, murder, and illegitimate childbirth by another man's wife. Yes, David failed—and failed miserably—but God forgave him and still had a plan for his life.

David's bleeding heart spoke a language that only God could understand.

What the enemy had intended for evil was a blessing in disguise.

Joseph

Joseph's bleeding, which lasted from the age of 17 to the age of 30, involved his being ridiculed, hated, rejected, thrown into a pit, sold as a slave, held in a dungeon, falsely accused, thrown into prison, and forgotten. At the right time, however, God raised him from the pit to the pinnacle.

In order for Joseph to fulfill God's dream for his life, he had to come into contact with certain people. In fact, every hard place in Joseph's life was a divine imperative. At the same time, God blessed Joseph at every place along the way. What the enemy had intended for evil was a blessing in disguise.

Remember, no matter what you are going through—no matter where you are in life—the truth of Romans 8:28 is yours to claim. God is causing your circumstances to work together for your good.

> *And we know that all things work together for good to them that love God, to them who are the called according to his purpose. Romans 8:28*

When shepherds bleed, God always has a higher purpose in mind—one that affects not only the life of the shepherd but the lives of those in his flock—and maybe even the entire nation.

A Place Called "Yes"

It is a medically proven fact that the blood type of children is determined by the seed of the father. Jesus' blood came from the seed of His Father and was conceived without an earthly father through the womb of a virgin. His was the blood of Immanuel–God with us.

In the Garden of Gethsemane, Jesus' sweat became as great drops of blood (Luke 22:39-44).

> *And being in an agony he prayed more earnestly: and his sweat was as it were great drops of blood falling down to the ground. Luke 22:44*

As His blood fell to the ground, it cried out with a language that God understood. Finally, Jesus was able to say, "Not my will, but thine, be done" (Luke 22:42), and an angel was sent to strengthen Him.

You may be bleeding as you agonize and wrestle in the Gethsemane of your ministry. Your heart bleeds with the desire to say "yes" to God and "no" to self. You may have prayed once, but you must keep praying until Gethsemane becomes a place called "yes" for you.

You must keep praying until Gethsemane becomes a place called "yes" for you.

If you are bleeding in the place where you are struggling, don't give up. Like Jesus' disciples, your prayer warriors may have gone to sleep, but don't let that stop you. I know it is hard. I know it is painful. I know it is lonely.

Go ahead and agonize; go ahead and bleed. Stay in your Gethsemane until your will dies and God can transfuse His will into your life. Your blood is speaking a language that only God understands: "Not my will but thine be done."

A Language Only God Understands

Isaiah prophesied that Jesus would be beaten when he wrote, "I gave my back to those who struck me" (Isaiah 50:6). As the 39 stripes were laid on Him, His back became like a newly plowed field, and Jesus' blood cried out, "By these stripes you are healed" (John 19:34).

Jesus' blood is crying out today, speaking better things than that of Abel (Hebrews 12:24).

As the soldier took a spear and pierced Jesus' side, out came blood and water. The water is symbolic of the tears you as a pastor have shed. Let that give you hope.

While no one can see the tears of a broken and bleeding heart, your blood is crying out. God is not One to forget your labor of love. Your blood, your heart, and your tears speak a language God understands.

There are some cries that only God can interpret.

> *For ye have not received the spirit of bondage again to fear; but ye have received the Spirit of adoption, whereby we cry, Abba, Father . . . For we know that the whole creation groaneth and travaileth in pain together until now. And not only they, but ourselves also, which have the firstfruits of the Spirit, even we ourselves groan within ourselves, waiting for the adoption, to wit, the redemption of our body . . . Likewise the Spirit also helpeth our infirmities: for we know not what we should pray for as we ought: but the Spirit itself maketh intercession for us with groanings which cannot be uttered.*
>
> *Romans 8:15, 22, 23, 26*

In these verses, there are three groans and one cry that only God can understand.

The word "cry" in Romans 8:15 means to scream out in a shrill voice, or to shriek. The word "groan" in verses 22, 23, and 26, means to speak or moan in a common language; to speak as one who can associate with your dilemma.

God can relate to your dilemma because you are in covenant relationship with Him. At times, you simply need to crawl up into the lap of the Father and cry, "I need you, Abba Father."

Before a child learns to speak, he cries. His mother takes the infant's whining gibberish and makes sense of the language. That is exactly what the Holy Ghost does when your heart is broken.

The Holy Spirit will make groans in a heavenly language that only God understands. It confuses the devil because it bypasses his intellect and vocabulary–but God understands.

No matter how deep, sweet, clear, cool, or refreshing a body of water may be, if there is no outlet, it will become stagnant, bitter, and of no use at all. It will become like the Dead Sea, which has many inlets but no outlets and is of no use.

There are some $30 trillion worth of natural resources trapped in the Dead Sea, all of which have no way of being used. They are trapped in a dilemma with no way out.

Your tears are your outlet. When you cry, your tears are released to God and they speak a language that God understands.

When Life Returns

In Genesis 1:2, the earth was *hayah*, meaning it became void, empty, and in chaos.

> *And the earth was without form, and void; and darkness was upon the face of the deep. And the Spirit of God moved upon the face of the waters. Genesis 1:2*

The earth wasn't always this way. After the fall of Satan, the earth changed from its original form–filled with life and vegetation and everything a perfect God could create–to something dead.

Satan tried to kill and abort the ministry of creation, but the Spirit of God brooded over the earth, as a hen over her nest of eggs. In six days, everything Satan meant for evil was turned to good. God said, "Let it be," and it was so.

In Genesis 2:7, we read that Adam was shaped, molded, and squeezed into a form but had no life.

And the Lord God formed man of the dust of the ground, and breathed into his nostrils the breath of life; and man became a living soul. Genesis 2:7

Then something happened, and Adam became a living soul. That word, "became," is also the Hebrew word *hayah*.

God breathed into Adam the breath of life, and the form became living. All God must do is show up and breathe upon something that is just a form, without a purpose, and it suddenly becomes alive. It becomes something fresh and vibrant, able to function, and to bring about change.

Abel's blood cried out because death caused Abel to go back to the ground (Hebrew word Adam). Abel was going back to only a form of what God had planned him to be. The life had drained out of him.

Your blood is crying out against mediocrity, against powerlessness, against lukewarmness. It is crying out against dead forms and dead motions. Your blood is crying, "Don't go back to what you were before the Holy Ghost breathed into you the power and ability to change."

Like Abel, you may be bleeding because of jealous "brothers" who can't stand the fact that God is blessing you. They have already dug your grave, but your blood is crying out. You may be a bleeding shepherd, but before you and your ministry return to the ground–to just a dead image of who and what God intended–cry out!

Maybe you are already in the grave, and jealousy is throwing the dirt over your remains. Your blood will speak a language that God understands. Just as He did with Abel, God will give you a stronger ministry. Inside you is a Seth to take the place of Abel, whom jealousy murdered.

Maybe you are like Joseph. You have a dream; you are impregnated with a ministry. Your own family, the members of your congregation, or your fellow ministers have risen up against you. You have been ridiculed and forgotten, but you have continued to serve God in the pit.

Get ready. You, like Joseph, have bled long enough! God is going to promote you above your tormentors.

Maybe you are like David. You have made mistakes; you would like to roll back time and turn back the clock. You long to undo your past, but it seems to be too late. Doors have been closed to you, and those whom you looked to for refuge have failed you. Your bleeding heart is crying out as did David's, "My sin is ever before me."

You Need a Transfusion

In the physical realm, the very life of our bodies is totally dependent upon blood. "For the life of the flesh is in the blood" (Leviticus 17:11).

We can lose an arm, a hand, an eye or a leg and still live, but if we lose the blood that sustains our lives, we will die.

Bleeding, however, has a positive effect. When we are wounded, the wound opens up an avenue for the blood to flush out any contaminants that would otherwise cause infection.

Of course, when a person is bleeding, the bleeding must be stopped and the wound sutured with stitches so that the healing process can take place.

Sometimes people have bled for so long that they need a transfusion of blood. For their bodies to function again, their blood count must be brought back up to its original level. The person who supplies the blood for the transfusion must have the same blood type. Otherwise, the body of the wounded person will reject the blood, and this can be fatal.

You have brothers and sisters in the Lord with your blood type. Instead of condemning you, they will pour out their blood for you. Why? Because they, too, have failed.

It is usually those who, in the past, have needed a transfusion themselves who are the first to donate blood when, in an emergency, someone is wounded and dying. These donors are willing to bleed themselves so someone else can live.

Allow your brothers and sisters in Christ to bind up your wounds, give you a transfusion, and begin the process of healing in your life.

Refuse to Go Back

Are there areas in your ministry that you refuse to allow to die? I know that you have been wounded. I know that your wounds have run deep. I know that the struggle has been great, but something is crying out in you as mediocrity and low self-esteem beckons for excellence.

You need to push forward and make your appeal to God. Refuse to go back to the dead form from which God has brought you. What does it matter if chaos reigns and certain areas of your life are in disarray and in discord? Continue your push for excellence, continue your appeal to be everything God has ordained you to be.

The real life, your very blood, cries out, "I refuse to go back to being just a form–what I was before God breathed on me."

If God has given you a ministry, know that He doesn't give ministries and then take them away (Romans 11:29). God sees your blood; He will be faithful to give you another chance.

God never chooses to use anyone greatly whom He has not first allowed to be hurt deeply.

Questions

1. Explain what God meant when He said, the "blood crieth unto me from the ground." _____

_____

_____

_____

2. Write the cry of your heart. _____

_____

_____

_____

3. Over the past year has your ministry gone forward or backward with God? Explain why. _____

_____

_____

_____

4. With whom do you identify most–Abel, Moses, David, or Joseph? Explain why. _____

_____

_____

_____

5. Have there been times in your ministry when you could relate to

Jesus' agony in Gethsemane? Explain your struggle and how it changed your life._____

_____

_____

_____

6. Describe a time when God ministered to you in a time of deep distress._____

_____

_____

_____

7. Name some things in your ministry that you need to pray about in a language (in tongues) that only God can understand._____

_____

_____

_____

8. According to John 19:34, what does the water gushing out of Jesus' side represent? How does this relate to you as a wounded shepherd?__

_____

_____

_____

_____

9. How did the breath of God change Adam? How can God's Spirit change you?_____

_____

_____

_____

10. Are there any "jealous brothers" in your life? If so, have you forgiven them?_____

_____

_____

_____

11. Have you ever been a spiritual "blood donor" for someone else? Explain why or why not._____

_____

_____

_____

12. What beckons for excellence in your life? Explain what you must do to restore life to your ministry._____

_____

_____

_____

Notes

Notes

Notes

Getting a Second Opinion

I n light of the added responsibilities that pastors face today, you probably need new life infused and transfused into your being, your ministry, your family, and your church.

As a senior pastor for several years, I have learned many valuable lessons. Some brought joy while others resulted in deep wounds that bled relentlessly for years and nearly killed me.

I thought it was a sign of weakness for a pastor to need prayer or help. Instead of trying to find someone with whom I could share my burden, I kept my hurts in the safety deposit box of my soul. People saw me smiling and outwardly healthy, but inwardly, I was literally bleeding. I was losing blood, dying a silent but very sure death.

When I was 27 years old, a doctor told me that I had the body of a fifty-year-old man and that I would not live to see my thirtieth birthday. Shaken by the thought of only three years to live, I had to move quickly. It was time to do something definite.

Lying in my hospital bed with my body too weak to move, every demon from hell's army waged a war against my mind. Satan came to me and told me that I would die and not live.

I closed the door to my hospital room and got down on my knees. "Lord," I prayed, "I need some answers. The doctor says I'm a dead man just looking for a grave. Satan attacks my mind, urging me to give it up and to throw in the towel. I need your help! I can't wait any longer. Time is running out!"

There in that hospital room, the Holy Ghost spoke and said, "You have a right to a second opinion! You do not have to accept the prognosis of man or the devil!"

If you need immediate attention, if you are bleeding profusely, I have good news. You don't have to fill out funeral papers for your ministry; you do not have to give burial rights to your goals, your dreams, your ambitions. You do not have to abort the baby you are carrying. All you need is a second opinion.

"You have a right to a second opinion!"

Before the Final Verdict

If you have medical tests done and the results come back positive, your doctor will oftentimes call in a specialist to get a second opinion.

In the judicial system, if the defendant is not satisfied with the final verdict, he has the right to appeal the decision. The defendant can ask for a retrial before the court of appeals.

In Revelation 12:10, Satan is called the accuser who accuses us before the throne of God day and night.

The word "accuse" here means to slander; to oppose with intention of holding one down; to seize and lay hold on; or to prevent one from reaching his full potential.

How does Satan accuse us? In four ways:

1. He will slander us before God (Revelation 12:10).

2. He will slander us to ourselves. "My sin is ever before me" (Psalm 51:2,3b).

3. He will accuse us to others. "Where are thine accusers" (John 8:10).

4. He will try to accuse God by saying to us, "If God loved you, then you wouldn't be going through what you are going through."

God, however, has made a way for us to appeal our case. If we sin, if we miss the mark of God, we are not arbitrarily condemned. Our cases are heard before the throne of heaven.

> *If we confess our sins, he is faithful and just to forgive us our sins, and to cleanse us from all unrighteousness. If we say that we have not sinned, we make him a liar, and his word is not in us. My little children, these things write I unto you, that ye sin not. And if any man sin, we have an advocate with the Father, Jesus Christ the righteous: And he is the propitiation for our sins: and not for ours only, but also for the sins of the whole world. 1 John 1:9-2:2*

We have an advocate–one who has been called to help with our case. This Advocate, while our own good deeds may be unacceptable, becomes "the propitiation"–that which causes us to become acceptable before God.

Change Your Focus

Like many of you, the woman with the "issue of blood" (Mark 5:25-34) faced a twofold dilemma.

First and foremost, she was bleeding to death. It was a silent death, but yet it was very definite. Each day, she felt herself getting weaker and weaker. Her second problem was just as serious. She had no one to help her.

And a certain woman, which had an issue of blood twelve years, And had suffered many things of many physicians, and had spent all that she had, and was nothing bettered, but rather grew worse. Mark 5:25,26

Leviticus 15:1-28 explains the law concerning anyone with an issue of blood. Verse 19 says that "she shall be put apart." This woman's problem had isolated her not only from society but from her family and friends. She could not go into the congregation of the righteous (church functions). It was a very lonely time for her.

According to the Law, if anyone touched her, they became "unclean." If she became tired and sat down next to someone, she would hear the person scream, "Unclean!"

In her dreams at night she would hear the word, "Unclean." Wherever she went, she heard people whispering and gossiping about her condition, making her feel dirty and inferior to others.

The Law put this woman on a seven day probation—after seven days "she shall be clean" (Leviticus 15:28).

In the Bible, the number seven denotes completion, perfection, the end of a matter. No doubt, this woman would count the days. Day one, she was thankful to get through, but by the sixth day, just when she thought she had things whipped, she would feel the pain. She would experience the uncontrollable bleeding.

The people would then separate themselves, and as she was once again isolated and ridiculed, her sense of inferiority became even deeper and more hurtful. She was dying, bleeding to death, yet she had no one to turn to for help or comfort.

After 12 years of false illusions and dashed hopes, she left her doctors and decided to get a second opinion.

When she had heard of Jesus, came in the press behind, and touched his garment. For she said, If I may touch but his clothes, I shall be whole. Mark 5:27,28

"When she had heard of Jesus," she immediately put aside all her fears.

This woman's greatest fear had become her greatest need. The one thing she wasn't supposed to do was the very thing she ultimately had to do. The Law said, "Do not touch anyone or anything." When this woman came to Jesus, however, she chose to forget the word, "unclean."

She chose to break the rules and to rehearse these words: "If I may touch but his clothes, I shall be whole."

Her focus changed from what people thought of her to what Jesus could do for her. She set her eyes on the hem of Jesus' garment.

The hem of a garment is the part where all the loose ends meet and are tied together. It is the part of a garment that holds everything together that would otherwise unravel. It keeps the garment from falling apart.

You have a life, a ministry, a gift, a calling, maybe even a marriage that is unraveling. Because of an issue that caused you to bleed, it now has gotten so bad that your life, your ministry, your marriage is coming apart at the seams.

It is time for you to touch the hem of Jesus' garment. He can suture the wound, stop the bleeding, and infuse and transfuse new life and healing into your very being.

Reach Out and Break the Rules

On the day that this woman entered the crowd, many other people were accidentally brushing up against Jesus. This woman, however, came with a desire to detach herself from the issue that was out of control and to attach herself to the hem of a garment that would make everything all right.

And straightway the fountain of her blood was dried up; and she felt in her body that she was healed of that plague. And Jesus, immediately knowing in himself that virtue had gone out of him, turned him about in the press, and said, Who touched my clothes? And his disciples said unto him, Thou seest the multitude thronging thee, and sayest thou, Who touched me? And he looked round about to see her that had done this thing. But the woman fearing and trembling, knowing what was done in her, came and fell down before him, and told him all the truth. And he said unto her, Daughter, thy faith hath made thee whole; go in peace, and be whole of thy plague.
Mark 5:29-34

As she touched Him, Jesus was moved. He felt 12 years of brokenness, 12 years of waiting, isolation, loneliness, and despair. He was so moved by her touch that He just touched her back. He touched her until her issue subsided; He touched her until she felt it.

The word "touch" actually means one who can relate to you by going through what you are going through. Hebrews 4:14-16 tells us that Jesus is "touched with the feeling of our infirmities." Infirmities are our weaknesses or inability to produce results. Jesus is touched because when you bleed, He bleeds—we are His body.

Seeing then that we have a great high priest, that is passed into the heavens, Jesus the Son of God, let us hold fast our profession. For we have not an high priest which cannot be touched with the feeling of our infirmities; but was in all points tempted like as we are, yet without sin. Let us therefore come boldly unto the throne of grace, that we may obtain mercy, and find grace to help in time of need.
Hebrews 4:14-16

Before you allow fate to slam the gavel of man's opinion down against you, and before you call the family of God around your bedside to relinquish your calling and ministry, you need to get a second opinion.

Make your appeal to Jesus because He is your Counselor; He is the Great Physician. Even if what they say about you is true, He is a God of second chances. Did He not give David a second chance? Did He not give Peter a second chance?

Jesus is touched because when you bleed, He bleeds–we are His body.

Come now, Jesus stands on the shores of your destiny. He has built a fire. He still gives the invitation, "Come and Dine." He knows how it hurts. He sees your bleeding, and He knows that your problems have become real issues.

> *But when the morning was now come, Jesus stood on the shore: but the disciples knew not that it was Jesus. Then Jesus saith unto them, Children, have ye any meat? They answered him, No. And he said unto them, Cast the net on the right side of the ship, and ye shall find. They cast therefore, and now they were not able to draw it for the multitude of fishes. Therefore that disciple whom Jesus loved saith unto Peter, It is the Lord. Now when Simon Peter heard that it was the Lord, he girt his fisher's coat unto him, (for he was naked,) and did cast himself into the sea. John 21:4-7*

Like the woman with the issue of blood, Peter was desperate and knew this was his time to act. He "plunged into the sea" without testing the temperature or the depth of the water. He didn't care what the other fishermen thought of him. He needed what Jesus had to offer, and he needed it immediately.

Sometimes you have to reach out and break the rules. Don't worry about what other people think of you. Your destiny is in your own hands, you have the right to a second opinion.

1. Explain the part of the Counselor in Isaiah 9:6 as the verse relates to getting a second opinion._____

_____

_____

_____

2. Who is the source of all accusations and indictments against your ministry?_____

_____

_____

_____

3. What are the four ways that Satan accuses you? Give a specific example of each from your own life._____

_____

_____

_____

_____

_____

4. What is an advocate and why do you need one?_____

_____

_____

_____

5. What was the twofold dilemma of the woman with the issue of blood in Mark 5?_____

_____

_____

_____

6. Name five areas in your life that have become uncontrollable "issues."_____

_____

_____

_____

7. How did this woman change her focus?_____

_____

_____

_____

8. Where is your focus today and how should you change it?_____

_____

_____

_____

9. What was the difference between the touch of this woman and Jesus' contact with the crowd?_____

_____

_____

_____

10. How can suppressing your feelings and hurts end up being detrimental to you?_____

_____

_____

_____

11. What "rules" or opinions are holding you back from reaching out and touching Jesus?_____

_____

_____

_____

12. Are you desperate enough to reach out and break the rules? If so, explain what that will mean in your life._____

_____

_____

_____

Notes

Notes

Notes

A Shepherd's Best Friend

bout ten years ago, I had the opportunity to meet a real Middle Eastern shepherd in the Cedron Valley of Jerusalem.

During a ten day pastors' tour, I experienced things I could never have learned in a lifetime of mere study. The trip came at a point in my life when I was almost burned out. In fact, I had planned this trip for rest, relaxation, and replenishment.

One evening, God led me to sit down on a tall, back wall outside my motel room. The sun was just beginning to set as evening was drawing near. Just a trace of sunlight remained when I looked deep into the Cedron Valley.

The sound of an echoing voice caught my attention. Then I saw a sight that humbled me and brought tears to my eyes. A shepherd was making his way up the valley toward a large sheepfold fenced in by a rock wall. This would be the place where he, along with his flock, would reside for the night.

This old, gray-headed, wrinkle-faced, and somewhat stooped shepherd stood up, and in Hebrew, let out a loud cry that echoed into the depths of the Cedron Valley. Immediately, approximately 100 animals, a mixture of lambs and some goats, lifted their heads in response to the voice. Then the shepherd sat down and waited as the motley herd lined up and walked toward him.

As I watched, I was reminded of the words of Jesus, "My sheep hear my voice, and I know them, and they follow me" (John 10:27).

For several minutes I watched the sheep and lambs until, out of the corner of my eye, I caught movement near the old gray-headed shepherd. To my surprise, I noticed two dogs, one on each side of him right at his heels.

As the shepherd made his way through the rough and rugged terrain, I observed that he limped and could only walk a short distance before he had to stop and rest for a moment. As he grew closer, I could see that his hands and feet were scarred and bleeding.

I asked the Lord, "Where did this bleeding, those scars and wounds, come from?"

As I pondered that question, I received the answer in living color. As the shepherd was waiting for his sheep and lambs to come up the valley, he bowed down on his knees to remove thorns from the path. In this part of Israel, the thorn plants grow low to the ground and have two-inch long spikes.

Knowing those thorns would have wounded and scarred the sheep and lambs, the shepherd cleared them away from the path. He was wounded and bleeding because of his love for the flock.

The Shepherd's Best Friends

You have heard it said, "A dog is man's best friend." This might be a figure of speech to some, but this shepherd knew the truth of that statement.

In fact, what I observed next changed my life forever.

When the old shepherd sat down to rest, the two dogs licked his bleeding hands and feet. They got up in his lap, and the old shepherd took them in his arms and held them close being careful not to show more attention to one than to the other.

As I sat watching, God ministered a word to my heart that became a breath of fresh air and a refreshing drink of water through the blistering sun of my fiery trials. The message the Lord conveyed to me is the message I hope to convey to you–God's shepherds.

He said, "These dogs are this shepherd's best friends." He said, "When no one else is around, when no one else cares to listen or understand, he can find, in them, friends."

The Lord then directed my eyes toward the flock and asked me, "Who else does this shepherd have? The sheep are afar off and can't understand him. The lambs are too immature; they could never understand his hurts and his bleeding. The other shepherds have their own problems. Besides there is such competition among the shepherds that they have no compassion for one another. He has no one else to talk to except his two dogs."

I just sat there and wept like a baby. I wanted to walk away, but God would not allow me to.

I sat there and through tear-rimmed eyes watched this old shepherd get up and speak in Hebrew to the two dogs. I don't know what was said, but the dogs knew, for they responded immediately and ran with the speed of an antelope down the valley. Apparently, they knew exactly where they were going.

With swiftness and much confidence, the two dogs ran down the valley toward the flock that was scattered. One dog on each side of the valley herded up the sheep and lambs that had not responded to the voice of the shepherd. The two dogs worked in conjunction with each other, circling around the sheep and lambs.

As the sheep and lambs began to move closer to the shepherd, the dogs would periodically bark. Some of the flock refused to respond to the shepherd's voice or the barking of the dogs, and they were still scattered across the valley. The two dogs began, ever so slightly, to nip at the heels of the wandering sheep and lambs.

Those two dogs, along with the voice of the shepherd, herded up the flock and moved them toward safe confines before darkness fell. They were very patient so as to not alarm the timid sheep, but they were very persistent.

Then in the midst of this gathering, the shepherd, as an act of gratitude, took the dogs up in his arms before his flock as if to say, "These two dogs are my nearest and dearest friends. They are your best friends, too. For, before darkness falls, I must get you safely inside the fold. These two dogs lovingly followed you and protected you until you were safely by my side."

Only when the flock lay down inside the fold did the old shepherd sit–in the doorway. This was his way of saying, "I will protect you. If anything is to get to you, it must first come through me."

Then the two dogs positioned themselves on either side of the shepherd. They cuddled up to him as if to say, "We are here first to be your friend and companion, then, at your command, to be a friend to the flock."

What Is a Friend?

Job calls his sheep-herding friends, "The dogs of my flock" (Job 30:1).

The shepherd, David, named his two dogs, "Goodness and Mercy" (Psalm 23:6) and described their purpose–"They shall follow me"–and the certainty of their companionship–"surely." David also knew the persistence of his two dogs–"They shall follow me all the days of my life."

God's two sheep dogs meet all the criteria of a true friend.

Let's look at four truths God's Word teaches us about friends:

1. God can, and God wants to be, your friend (James 2:23).

2. A true friend will love at all times–not just when things are going well, but when you hurt and bleed. As a shepherd, you need the friends that God gives to love you and help to lick away your pain (Proverbs 17:17; Luke 16:21).

3. In many cases, your family may be the ones who most misunderstand your commitment to God. In those times God says, I will give you a friend who will stick "closer than a brother" (Proverbs 18:24).

4. Solomon says that a friend's wounds are "faithful" (Proverbs 27:6). This word, faithful, means to be firm; to build up; to support by taking one by the right hand. It also means to cause one to be established.

Many feel that a friend is someone who will go along with you and even compromise the truth. According to this verse, however, a true friend, because of his commitment to righteousness, will recognize the wrong, take you by the hand, and lead you into truth. His admonitions may wound you, but this kind of wound will cause you to stand and be established.

You see, it isn't bad to bleed when you are wounded if the bleeding is controlled. This is God's way of purging your wound of contaminants that would cause infection.

"Goodness and Mercy" will be true friends to you. They will allow you to take off your blood-spotted garments to expose your wounds and your hurts.

"Goodness and Mercy" will be true friends to you.

Time to Move Out of the Cave

You have a word from God, but because of fear and intimidation, like Elijah, you have secluded yourself into your own little prison.

On the outside of your cave of seclusion and withdrawal there is a Jehu, a Hazael, an Elisha whom God intends for you to infuse with an anointing. Yet, you are the one who needs an infusion. You are bleeding because of your own feelings of inadequacy and your own complex of inferiority.

This is exactly what Elijah felt as he realized the great task laid before him (I Kings 15:13-14). He got waylaid from the path of God.

When you, like Elijah—because of the fear of failure, insecurity, and intimidation—begin to withdraw into a cave of seclusion, "Goodness and Mercy" will visit you. They will come with a whisper and not with boisterous and ferocious barks of condemnation.

> *And he came thither unto a cave, and lodged there; and, behold, the word of the Lord came to him, and he said unto him, What doest thou here, Elijah? And he said, I have been very jealous for the Lord God of hosts: for the children of Israel have forsaken thy covenant, thrown down thine altars, and slain thy prophets with the sword; and I, even I only, am left; and they seek my life, to take it away. And he said, Go forth, and stand upon the mount before the Lord. And, behold, the Lord passed by, and a great and strong wind rent the mountains, and brake in pieces the rocks before the Lord; but the Lord was not in the wind: and after the wind an earthquake; but the Lord was not in the earthquake: And after the earthquake a fire; but the Lord was not in the fire: and after the fire a still small voice. 1 Kings 19:9-12*

The voice Elijah needed to hear came in a whisper, and so it will be with you.

Goodness will crawl up on your lap and lick your wounds. Then he will look you right in the face and whisper, "I had fainted had I not believed to see the goodness of God" (Psalm 27:13).

Your other friend, Mercy, will crawl up and cuddle beside you licking your wounds and ever so softly whisper, "I have your back covered. I have followed you, and I haven't come this far to leave you now." Remember that God "sheweth mercy to his anointed" and "his mercy endureth forever" (Psalm 18:50; Psalm 106:1).

These two dogs, Goodness and Mercy, are God's faithful friends to you. Learn about them, know them, talk to them, trust and depend on them.

As soon as you are healed, however, it is time to move on. You will be sent back into the fields. Like Elijah, God will bring you out of your cave so you can bring anointing to your own sheep.

> *And the Lord said unto him, Go, return on thy way to the wilderness of Damascus: and when thou comest, anoint Hazael to be king over Syria: And Jehu the son of Nimshi shalt thou anoint to be king over Israel: and Elisha the son of Shaphat of Abel-meholah shalt thou anoint to be prophet in thy room. 1 Kings 19:15-16*

Within your flock, there sits a Hazael, a Jehu, or an Elisha that God will anoint through your leadership. Once God has ministered to you, it is time to get up and get back on the job.

Befriended by Goodness and Mercy

When David became a leader for God, he immediately came into covenant relationship with Jonathan, the son of King Saul (I Samuel 18:1). The two cut themselves and then touched blood to blood, wound to wound.

In I Samuel 18:1, we learn that the very soul of Jonathan was knit with the soul of David. The Hebrew word for "knit" in this verse means to tie, to bind, to lace together, or to intertwine with unbreakable cords.

This is what Goodness and Mercy want to do. When you come into covenant with Goodness and Mercy, they will bring you into an understanding of God's love that will cause you to be unshakable and unmovable.

A careful study of David and Jonathan reveals the kind of relationship Goodness and Mercy wish to have with you:

1. They want to knit up the loose ends of insecurity in your life.

2. They want an intimate closeness with you in the agape love of God.

3. They want to make a covenant with you to follow you all the days of your life. Their agreement is secure and cannot be broken. They have touched your hurt, and your hurt touches them.

4. They want to have an open relationship with you that will allow you to be who you are without fear of rejection. They want you to be able to totally strip yourself of all your complexes, your fears, your failures–right down to the very worst thing about you.

5. Goodness and Mercy want to share your strengths. In a covenant relationship, your weaknesses and your strengths are intertwined.

6. Finally, Goodness and Mercy will allow you to be truthful, and they will be truthful with you. A person who will not

tell you the truth has no true interest in your well-being. Goodness and Mercy will always be truthful with you and allow you to share with them your "girdle"–the truth about you.

Come into covenant with Goodness and Mercy as David did with Jonathan. Goodness and Mercy will allow you to strip yourself. As you share your weakness with them, they will also allow you to share your sword and bow of strengths. They will allow you to share the girdle of truth as you are open and let the wounds bleed.

Goodness and Mercy Are Tracking You

You are being tracked. You have been redeemed by God's own blood, and when God's shepherds bleed, His two bloodhounds will track the trail of blood.

Goodness and Mercy are the very essence of God's nature and exemplify His very attributes. As sheep, your very tracks are leaving a scent that the character and nature of God recognizes.

Listen for the sounds of Goodness and Mercy. Do you feel them nipping at your heels?

Goodness says to a bleeding shepherd, "You would have fainted if it were not for me. I have caused you to feel remorse, but it is to show you that even in your dilemma, God's goodness is there to lead you to repentance" (Romans 2:4).

I had fainted, unless I had believed to see the goodness of the Lord in the land of the living. Psalm 27:13

Now listen to Mercy as his bark works in conjunction with Goodness. Hear Mercy barking out, "The mercy of the Lord is following you. I am the very essence of God. I will never leave you; I will never forsake you" (Hebrews 13:5).

Just when the enemy takes you to a place where wrong looks

right, Goodness barks out. Just when you feel you have gone too far, Mercy begins to yelp, "I know where you are! I know your downsitting! I know your uprising!"

> *O Lord, thou hast searched me, and known me. Thou knowest my downsitting and mine uprising, thou understandest my thought afar off. Thou compassest my path and my lying down, and art acquainted with all my ways. For there is not a word in my tongue, but, lo, O Lord, thou knowest it altogether. Thou hast beset me behind and before, and laid thine hand upon me. Psalm 139:1-5*

Goodness and Mercy work together just to let you know you can make it! We have a Shepherd who goes before us. Why? Because shepherds don't drive; they lead.

God's two sheep dogs are there whenever my wounds are saying, "The pain is too much to bear;" when discouragement suggests, "Give it up;" when past failures and mistakes demand, "Go back!"

It is then that you hear the echoes of your shepherd saying, "Follow me." But your past is calling out, "You will never make it." Your mistakes have already made funeral arrangements for your ministry.

> *Whither shall I go from thy spirit? or whither shall I flee from thy presence? If I ascend up into heaven, thou art there: if I make my bed in hell, behold, thou art there. If I take the wings of the morning, and dwell in the uttermost parts of the sea; Even there shall thy hand lead me, and thy right hand shall hold me. Psalm 139:7-10*

But wait . . . I hear barking in the distance. I can't see them, but I hear their barks getting closer. It's as though they know where I am.

As I look back at the drops along my path, I see the reason I am being pursued by these two dogs. They know the scent of my blood.

Your trail has been marked. Through every storm, every valley, you have been tracked. Why? For two reasons:

1. You are leaving the scent of a sheep.

2. Your very blood is of the same spiritual blood type as that of your Shepherd.

At the voice of His command, Goodness and Mercy have tracked your blood-sprinkled path, and the bleeding will stop.

Since Goodness and Mercy have followed you here, allow them to get up in your face, look you eye to eye, and lick your wounds. Allow them, like Norwegian Huskies, to carry your heavy cargo across the cold, barren terrain of your life. Let them be your best friends.

Listen to them when they say, He who has begun "a good work in you will perform it until the day of Jesus Christ" (Philippians 1:6).

The Path Before You

As you take inventory of your ministry and your walk with God, take note of the wounds, the bleeding, you have and are now experiencing. See the path that lies before you. It may be one that will require some painful decisions.

Remember, however, that you are not alone. You have a Shepherd who can relate to your pain and bleeding. Do not be afraid to be honest with God. You have nothing to prove to Him that He doesn't already know.

His two deputized dogs want to become your best friends. They want to help you, to give you companionship, to lick your wounds.

"Goodness and Mercy" will be your seeing-eye dogs when you cannot see which way to go. They will help you to retrieve certain gifts and talents that you may have thrown away in frustration. They will aid you in bearing those burdens in the cold, Arctic times of your life.

Finally, embrace Goodness. You will need his every whisper, and don't forget Mercy. He will sustain you because two sheep dogs really are a shepherd's best friends.

When you come into covenant with Goodness and Mercy, they will bring you into an understanding of God's love that will cause you to be unshakable and unmovable.

Questions

1. Name five things that a dog can do in the natural realm, that Goodness and Mercy are doing in your ministry in the spiritual realm._____

_____

_____

_____

2. List four characteristics of a true friend._____

_____

_____

_____

3. Do you have a friend who meets this criteria? Do you, as a friend, have these characteristics?_____

_____

_____

_____

4. Explain why Elijah was hiding in a cave._____

_____

_____

_____

5. List areas in your own ministry that make you want to run away and hide._____

_____

_____

_____

6. Within your flock, is there a Hazael, a Jehu, or an Elisha that God wants to anoint through your leadership? If so, name him or her._____

_____

_____

_____

7. In studying the relationship between Jonathan and David, discuss the significance of a blood covenant._____

_____

_____

_____

_____

8. Why is it not a good idea to share your hurts with the flock that you pastor?_____

_____

_____

_____

9. If you could, what would you do to enhance your relationship with God, with your spouse, and with your congregation to help stop your bleeding?_____

_____

_____

_____

10. What part do "Goodness and Mercy" play in the life of a bleeding and wounded shepherd?_____

_____

_____

_____

11. Write Psalm 139:1-5 in your own words._____

_____

_____

_____

_____

_____

_____

12. Describe how God's goodness and mercy have been tracking you._____

_____

_____

_____

Notes

Notes

Notes

Crossing Paths with the Good Samaritan

Several years ago, while in Jerusalem, I walked out on the Mount of Olives just as the sun was setting. I found a path that wound down toward a deep valley and the brook of Cedron. This was the path Jesus took on His way to the Garden of Gethsemane.

As I walked down this circling path, I saw a shepherd making his way up the rocky hillside leading to Jerusalem. I couldn't help but notice that this shepherd was limping.

I could tell by the grimace on his face that the shepherd was in obvious pain. As he walked closer, his limp became more noticeable.

Then, our paths crossed, and I stood eye to eye within inches of him. The shepherd's eyes cried out, as those of one who was very lonely and in need of companionship.

At this close proximity, I was able to see wounds on his body that were open and oozing out a fresh flow of blood.

What humbled me most, however, was noticing that some of his wounds were covered by his clothes. All I could see was a blood stain, signs of a wound disguised by layers of outer garments.

From this very moving experience with the old sheepherd, the Lord led me to draw several conclusions regarding God's shepherds and how we should relate to our flocks:

1. As God's under-shepherd, we have a path to walk if we are to get our flocks to the place where God wants them to be.

2. In walking this path, which is symbolic of God's sovereign will, there will be hurts that will cause us to bleed.

3. We may attempt to disguise our wounds, but wounds manifest themselves by an outward stain.

4. In order to see a person's disguised and innermost hurts, we have to walk in the path they are walking in.

In order to see a person's disguised and innermost hurts, we have to walk in the path they are walking.

Jesus' Inner Circle

Although multitudes of people followed the ministry of Jesus while He was on earth and walked where He walked, only twelve were among His closest associates.

We can compare Jesus' selection of his disciples to the way an incoming president handpicks his cabinet. These cabinet members then face a stiff interrogation by Congress where their life-styles, finances, and character come under close scrutiny. As their lives are examined, areas that, on the surface, were hidden become manifest.

Jesus handpicked His own cabinet (Mark 3:13-19).

And he goeth up into a mountain, and calleth unto him whom he would: and they came unto him. And he ordained twelve, that they should be with him, and that

he might send them forth to preach, And to have power to
heal sicknesses, and to cast out devils. Mark 3:13-15

Of those twelve, only three were allowed to cross paths with Him—paths of principle, purpose, and destiny. These three composed Jesus' inner circle. From a multitude of followers, Jesus found only three who were qualified to be an intimate part of His ministry: Peter, James, and John.

These three were allowed to see previews of His coming attractions on the Mount of Transfiguration (Matthew 17:1). They were allowed to go into the inner circle of Gethsemane to see their Shepherd bleed as He was pressed into the sovereign will of God.

These three were allowed to see things that the other nine were not. Jesus was very intimate with them as He poured His life and purpose into their spirits. Jesus had other disciples, but only three were allowed to experience the depths of His ministry and see His divine nature.

Out of those three, however, only one was able to go from the outer court (flesh), to the Holy place (soul), on into the Holy of Holies (Spirit) in Jesus' ministry—and that was John.

John, known as "the other disciple," leaned on Jesus' breast and listened for His every heartbeat. Called "the disciple whom Jesus loved," John was truly a man after God's heart, or innermost thoughts (John 21:20; Acts 13:22).

Only John recognized Jesus on the shore after His resurrection, and only John leaned upon Jesus after His resurrection. It was John who received the 22 chapters of Revelation that have altered the lives of thousands.

Only John wrote, "We have seen [Him] with our eyes," and "our hands have handled" Him (John 1:1).

Only John saw the wounds of a bleeding Shepherd as they stripped Him of His garment because, of the twelve, only he went to the cross. Only John was so close that he was to minister to Jesus' mother. Mary became as a mother to John, and John became as a son to Mary.

Allow me to relate these truths to you and your life as a shepherd:

1. Out of your congregation, there will be only a few you can allow to get close to you.

2. Out of the few, there may only be one whom you can allow to go into the very depths of your ministry.

Keep in mind that your life is scrutinized simply because of the office you hold. It is vitally important that you carefully select, as Jesus did, only those whom God reveals to you as your "three" or your "one".

Digressing From God's Pathway

God considers your ministry and your walk with Him as a very personal, private, and intimate matter. When you are bleeding, God takes special care to make sure you are cared for with compassion and sensitivity.

Jesus' story of the Good Samaritan provides simple yet powerful truths about bleeding shepherds left to die by the wayside.

> *And Jesus answering said, A certain man went down from Jerusalem to Jericho, and fell among thieves, which stripped him of his raiment, and wounded him, and departed, leaving him half dead. Luke 10:30*

Jesus said a "certain man" was traveling from Jerusalem to Jericho. Even though there were many walking along the Jericho road and headed in the same direction, Jesus saw this traveler as an individual–"a certain man."

Jesus had another reason for calling him "a certain man." In this story, Jesus left out all names so as to not belittle this man because of the path he walked. If you are a bleeding shepherd, you can rest assured that God will be careful to protect your identity.

You might be a Jacob now, but inside you there is an Israel. God may talk to you about your life, but until you have wrestled with who you are and have become who He wants you to be, He won't discuss your name.

God also holds your path—your walk and your direction—in the strictest of confidence.

Notice, however, that the man in Jesus' story "went down." I don't know why this man "went down" to Jericho. I don't know why he chose to leave Jerusalem. The fact that he was going down from Jerusalem to Jericho meant that his back was turned to one place and his heart toward another.

Jerusalem was the center of worship, the place of sacrifice. But the "certain man's" face and his heart were toward Jericho, which means a "luring fragrance." This man was being drawn away from Jerusalem to things that were going to cause him to bleed even further.

The road to Jericho was a steady decline. It didn't go straight down, it wound around 18 miles east of Jerusalem. The winding was one of steady digression and ultimately led to the Dead Sea.

The natural resources of the Dead Sea have gone down to the point of no return. They are beyond our reach. When we digress from God, the path always leads to a dead end.

You may be in a state of digression with God. By taking the path away from God, "the certain man" in Jesus' story caused five things to happen in his life:

1. He fell as he walked away from Jerusalem to Jericho.

2. His fall made him accessible to thieves (John 10:10).

3. He was stripped of his garment.

4. The fall among thieves brought about wounds that caused the man to bleed. This road was called "The Bloody Way."

5. He went away from Jerusalem and had his back turned away from God.

The course this man had taken caused him loneliness and despair as he was left to die all alone along the wayside.

You may be on the verge of a breakthrough. You may be one step away from a blessing, but walking away will cause you to fall among thieves. As you walk away from Jerusalem to Jericho, there is a robbery in progress. The devil is going to steal certain things from you.

The path away from God will strip you of your integrity, your virtue, and your power. It will strip you of everything you were ordained to receive.

When we digress from God, the path always leads to a dead end.

Adding Insult to Injury

As the bleeding man lay beaten by the wayside, "by chance there came down a certain priest that way: and when he saw him, he passed by on the other side" (verse 31).

The priest had no keen personal interest in this man and accidentally stumbled upon him. The priest saw that the man had fallen, but he was not surprised. After all, this very road was called a "bloody place." Afraid to get too close to the man, the priest never saw the bleeding wounds.

God help us, as His shepherds, not to be like the priest. May we never be found guilty of such complacency and lack of compassion. When we come across shepherds bleeding and fallen, may we do more than pass by on the other side as if we do not see.

This man was a high priest, and perhaps he did not want to become involved. Perhaps he cried out to the fallen, wounded, bleeding man from a distance, "I am on my way to the temple. I will pray for you."

It is easy to say, "I'll pray for you," when what bleeding pastors and shepherds sometimes really need is a spiritual transfusion.

Next, "a Levite" came by, but he took one look and crossed to the other side of the road.

And likewise a Levite, when he was at the place, came and looked on him, and passed by on the other side.

Luke 10:32

The fact that he was a Levite brings up several points:

1. He was very religious. The Levites were very conservative about the Law and made sure that the people lived by its statutes–at least outwardly.

2. At first, he positioned himself so that his path crossed that of the fallen man.

3. The Levite looked upon him and saw him fallen, stripped, wounded, and bleeding, but he showed no compassion.

4. He walked by on the other side.

As pastors and leaders, we must position ourselves in a place where we are able to see the wounds of others. We must pass by on the bleeding side not on the side that is covered up.

To offer only curious concern only adds insult to the pain of an injured brother or sister.

Where Are You?

Notice how the Samaritan reacted when he discovered the wounded and bleeding man who had been beaten, stripped, and cast by the wayside:

But a certain Samaritan, as he journeyed, came where he was: and when he saw him, he had compassion on him.

Luke 10:33

1. He came "where he was."

2. He not only came to where he was, but he also "saw him." You don't have to turn your injuries away from us, but you can turn your injuries to us. Let us see, because upon seeing, we will then know how to minister to you.

3. He "had compassion on him." He didn't see him with a legalistic and "holier than thou" attitude, but he tried to understand the man's pain.

As a result of the Samaritan's compassion, the fallen man accepted his help in spite of their cultural differences. Stripped, wounded, and bleeding, he figured that if this Samaritan thought enough to come to where he was, to who he was, to what he was–in all the blood and mess–then he must care.

Love will cover a multitude of sins. If you find a person who has your same blood type, who has been where you have been, has walked in your shoes, and has been saved by a blood transfusion themselves, then you can expose your wounds and let him see the worst. He didn't pass you by, so let him see the side that you covered up from others.

God wants to send someone where you are. If you are fallen, someone will come. If you are bleeding, someone will come. If you are of a different race, someone will come. It's up to you, however, to receive the one God sends across your path.

May God break down all barriers, whether religious or racial, and let us come together so we can bind up one another's wounds.

When Someone Crosses Your Path

What has wounded you? Is it other shepherds? Or are your wounds self inflicted?

Have you allowed your own fleshly appetites to hurt you? Do you feel that your wounds must not be exposed in fear of rejection? Have you been wounded by your own sheep and lambs?

The blood that is on you, is it yours or is it the blood of a little lamb that you held, comforting its quivering body through a trial or test?

Maybe you have merely had a surface healing, and it doesn't take much to reopen your yet infected wounds.

God will send someone across your path who will be like the Good Samaritan. He will do more than put a Band-Aid over your gaping lesions. He will stay around to see that you get the care you need until you are completely restored to full health.

And went to him, and bound up his wounds, pouring in oil and wine, and set him on his own beast, and brought him to an inn, and took care of him. And on the morrow when he departed, he took out two pence, and gave them to the host, and said unto him, Take care of him; and whatsoever thou spendest more, when I come again, I will repay thee. Luke 10:34-35

The person or people God sends to help you will do three things:

1. Bind up your wounds. No healing will ever occur as long as the wound is gaping open. It is important that the wound be closed up tightly. This stops any drainage, reduces swelling and prevents subsequent infection. Jesus

said in Luke 4:18, that one of the functions of the anointing is to "bind up the wounds." Let this be the beginning of a healing process that will allow you to reach your potential with God.

2. Bring healing. The Samaritan poured in oil, a type of the Holy Spirit–God's Healing Agent. Like oil, the Holy Spirit also serves as an antibiotic to cleanse out infection. If you are wounded, allow God to pour into you a fresh infilling of the Holy Spirit.

3. Take care of you. As the Samaritan took care of the wounded man, there are those in the Body of Christ who know how to minister and care for bleeding shepherds until they are completely healed.

As others reach out to you, do not turn them away. They must come near in order to see your hidden wounds. You may be fallen, stripped of your virtue and integrity.

While others have passed you by, you were able to conceal your wounds by not exposing them. God, however, is sending those to the other side, and they will see your wounds, pour in the Holy Spirit, and transfuse the blood of Jesus into your heart and mind so you can be healed.

Then, you can return to your Jerusalem ready to feed and tend your flock–because God has allowed your path to cross that of the Good Samaritan.

May God break down all barriers, whether religious or racial, and let us come together so we can bind up one another's wounds.

Questions

1. Are you walking where Jesus walked? Who else is walking on the same path with you?_____

_____

_____

_____

2. List those in your life who have become as the three, and as the one from the three._____

_____

_____

_____

_____

_____

3. Explain how God protects our identity and keeps our pathway in strictest confidence when we are bleeding._____

_____

_____

_____

4. What do the terms "Jerusalem" and "Jericho" represent in this particular chapter and how do they relate to your ministry?_____

_____

_____

_____

_____

5. Describe a time in your ministry, past or present, when you digressed from God's pathway and the consequences you suffered as a result._____

_____

_____

_____

6. Compare the different reactions made by the high priest and the Levite. _____

_____

_____

_____

7. Have there been times when you passed by on the other side of pastors in need? If so, why? What will you do differently in the future?_____

_____

_____

_____

8. In what ways do you feel others have passed by you on the other side?_____

_____

_____

_____

9. Are your wounds self inflicted or caused by others?_____

_____

_____

_____

10. Describe the response of the Samaritan and compare it to the way you reach out to wounded brothers and sisters._____

_____

_____

_____

11. If God sent someone across your path to minister to your needs, how would you respond? Would you be willing to expose your wounds?_____

_____

_____

_____

12. Why does God want to heal wounded shepherds? Why does God want to heal you?_____

_____

_____

_____

Notes

Notes

Notes

Finding Your Place of Refuge

One afternoon, I visited the shepherds' fields of Bethlehem in Judea, where Boaz met Ruth and Naomi. All around me were shepherds tending to their sheep and lambs. Some shepherds seemed energetic, while others appeared to be very weary. I walked over to a secluded and isolated place and quietly observed.

As I surveyed the scene before me, I realized the similarities that exist between a shepherd of sheep and the pastor of a church.

First, I noticed that everything they did came under close scrutiny. The flat fields, with not a tree in sight, allowed every move made by each shepherd to be visible to the others. If a shepherd fell, anyone could clearly see the fall because he was exposed. There was no place to hide. Even passersby, on their way to Jerusalem, could see everything that was taking place in the fields.

I also noticed that the shepherds had no shelter in a storm except for small cave-like dwellings. These, however, were merely small underpasses in the earth, only large enough for a shepherd and one wounded sheep or lamb.

Then it occurred to me that each shepherd—like the pastor—must bear the burden of any decisions he makes out in the field. If his decision was wrong, then he became a victim of his decision. His decisions affected not only himself but his entire flock.

In order for a shepherd to survive in this profession, his heart has to be in his work. To be effective, he has to become emotionally attached to those little lambs and sheep to the point where nothing else mattered.

As a pastor, you, too, are out in fields where everyone notices your every move. Other pastors may even see you when you fall. If you become injured and wounded, you may be able to cover up some of the bleeding, but the limp will still be noticeable.

Your heart may be crushed as you make decisions that will affect both you and your flock. While some decisions are good, others cause you to sit and weep as they make you their victim.

At times you may have to sit and hold the quivering, bleeding flesh of timid, frightened lambs while others sleep. As the blood of this little lamb leaves splotches of blood on your own garments, you may question "How long, oh Lord?"

As you crawl back into your cave, you long to seclude yourself from the storm raging all about you.

A Victim of the Storm

You may be a victim of the storm. Some of your storms may be self-made while others are beyond your control.

You may be bleeding and in need of attention. You have old wounds that have been covered up, yet the wounds are obvious because your garments are spotted with blood.

Maybe you were wounded by the sharp horns of a goat in your flock. No matter what the cause of your wounds and what your condition, you have a city of refuge.

In Psalm 142, we hear the lamenting cries of someone who was a shepherd himself. This time, however, David was on the other side of the fence. He was now taking his wounds to the Shepherd of his soul because he had become the victim of an attack against his spirit–his very life.

I cried unto the Lord with my voice; with my voice unto the Lord did I make my supplication. I poured out my complaint before him; I shewed before him my trouble. When my spirit was overwhelmed within me, then thou knewest my path. In the way wherein I walked have they privily laid a snare for me. I looked on my right hand, and beheld, but there was no man that would know me: refuge failed me; no man cared for my soul. I cried unto thee, O Lord: I said, Thou art my refuge and my portion in the land of the living. Attend unto my cry; for I am brought very low: deliver me from my persecutors; for they are stronger than I. Bring my soul out of prison, that I may praise thy name: the righteous shall compass me about; for thou shalt deal bountifully with me. Psalm 142

When David cried out that his "spirit was overwhelmed" (verse 3), he was saying, "I have come to the place where the walls are closing in. I see no way out, no escape, no refuge. I am a victim in a storm without any place to turn."

Have you gotten to the point where you are crying out to the Lord? If so, what are you going through that has brought you to tears? Is it the fact that you have fallen? Is it the fact that you are wounded? Do you cry because you don't have anyone you can talk to?

Remember, tears are a language God understands. Tears are God's way of releasing a flow inside you. Tears act as an outlet. As your tears flow, God is able to replenish you with fresh healing waters.

In verse 2, David says, "I poured out my complaint." In other words, David needed a place of refuge so he could replenish himself.

To replenish means to refill or to bring something back to its previous level or capacity. Areas of your life may need to be replenished. There is nothing wrong with needing replenishment. In fact, it testifies that you have been giving of yourself.

There is nothing wrong with needing replenishment. In fact, it testifies that you have been giving of yourself.

Lions and Snares

David needed a refuge from the feeling of entrapment. He calls it a "snare" in verse 3: "They have privily laid a snare for me."

As the shepherd in David's time surveyed the fields, he could see the flock being surrounded by animals waiting to devour the lambs or sheep. At night, though he couldn't see the wolves and lions, the shepherd could hear their movement and sense the uneasiness of his flock.

Sometimes the shepherd felt totally surrounded. It was his battle to fight, his decision to make.

David said in verse 4: "I looked on my right hand . . . but there was no man that would know me: refuge failed me." Overwhelmed by a feeling of loneliness, he said, "No man careth for my soul."

You may be struggling with your church, your marriage, or maybe with your number one enemy–yourself. You hear the gossip all around you and feel totally surrounded and stalked by Satan, who, like a roaring lion, is waiting to strike.

Lions roar because they are hungry. They also roar when they are intimidated. Satan sees your anointing and the power of God in your ministry. He knows that you are out to take your city, and he wants to make you back off. He saw you fall last week, so he goes throughout the shepherds' fields roaring out accusations against you.

Lions, however, will turn and flee if they are afraid, and there is one thing they fear. They fear a greater roar than their own.

When Satan roars against you and your flock, you need to remember that "greater is He that is in you, than he that is in the world." And since Jesus is greater, His roar is louder.

One of Christ's many attributes is that of the Lion of the tribe of Judah (Revelation 5:5), and when He roars, Satan must flee.

> *Be sober, be vigilant; because your adversary the devil, as a roaring lion, walketh about, seeking whom he may devour: Whom resist stedfast in the faith, knowing that the same afflictions are accomplished in your brethren that are in the world. But the God of all grace, who hath called us unto his eternal glory by Christ Jesus, after that ye have suffered a while, make you perfect, stablish, strengthen, settle you.* 1 Peter 5:8-10

What does Jesus roar? Three things:

A. As Lion of the Tribe of Judah, He roars out ruling authority.

B. As the Root of David, He roars out relationship. He can relate to what you are going through because He, too, was a man.

C. As the Lamb of God, He roars out reconciliation and redemption by His blood.

> *And I saw a strong angel proclaiming with a loud voice, Who is worthy to open the book, and to loose the seals thereof? And no man in heaven, nor in earth, neither under the earth, was able to open the book, neither to look thereon. And I wept much, because no man was found worthy to open and to read the book, neither to look there-on. And one of the elders saith unto me, Weep not: behold, the Lion of the tribe of Juda, the Root of David,*

hath prevailed to open the book, and to loose the seven seals thereof. And I beheld, and, lo, in the midst of the throne and of the four beasts, and in the midst of the elders, stood a Lamb as it had been slain, having seven horns and seven eyes, which are the seven Spirits of God sent forth into all the earth. Revelation 5:2-6

With the authority, relationship, and reconciliation of the Lion of Judah on your side, you have nothing to fear.

When You Make a Mistake

Before the people of Israel could come out of the desert and cross the Jordan River, they had to complete a series of lessons: Stop and Go; Sweetness out of Bitterness; Oasis in a Desert; Manna and Quail out of Nothing; From Self Government to God's Government. All of these experiences helped to bring Israel to Kadesh Barnea–the place of full submission.

Like the Israelites, you may be going through something you don't understand. You are being isolated and brought to loneliness because God wants you to see Him and no one else.

You look behind you and see the enemy pursuing you. You look before you and see the demands of a Red Sea ministry–one that seems to be unfathomable. Maybe you are going through bitter trials, dry places of doubt.

Maybe you are on Mount Sinai, where God is beginning to govern your life by the Word and not so much by a pillar of fire by night or a cloud by day. Whatever it is that you are experiencing, you can know that, if you stand the test, out of it will come bricks to build a city of refuge for others.

Before the Israelites could build cities of refuge, they had to cross the Jordan River and enter the land of Canaan.

And the Lord spake unto Moses, saying, Speak unto the children of Israel, and say unto them, When ye be come over Jordan into the land of Canaan; Then ye shall appoint you cities to be cities of refuge for you; that the slayer may flee thither, which killeth any person at unawares. And they shall be unto you cities for refuge from the avenger; that the manslayer die not, until he stand before the congregation in judgment. And of these cities which ye shall give six cities shall ye have for refuge. Ye shall give three cities on this side Jordan, and three cities shall ye give in the land of Canaan, which shall be cities of refuge. These six cities shall be a refuge, both for the children of Israel, and for the stranger, and for the sojourner among them: that every one that killeth any person unawares may flee thither. Numbers 35:9-15

These cities of refuge were established "for the children of Israel, for the stranger, and for the sojourner among them" (verse 15).

The "stranger" in this verse represents the sinner who needs a refuge. The "sojourner" is the person who has no real dwelling place. The "children of Israel" represent the people of God—Christians.

God designated these cities of refuge for people who had unwittingly or unintentionally harmed someone else. Certain things had happened that they did not premeditate or plan. They just simply made a mistake. They wished it hadn't happened; they would like to forget it, but there it is, haunting them everyday.

As if their own conscience and memory isn't bad enough, other shepherds out in the field have seen their fall. These fellow herdsmen are aware of their fallen comrades wounds and bleeding, but they fail to give refuge.

No one purposely brings harm to their ministry; it just happens. Like most pastors, you are the one who normally gives refuge to others. At times, however, you find yourself in need of refuge.

Run For Your Life

Some pastors will not reach their full potential until they deal with their mistakes. It may be immorality, unfaithfulness to your spouse, or an ungodly attitude. You may have a problem stemming from your childhood environment. Perhaps you feel intimidated and inferior to others, causing you to withdraw.

Numbers 35:11 explains that the victim in need of a refuge was trying to escape his accusers. He was to flee to the city—to run for his life.

A person running for his life doesn't have time to figure out where to go. He just needs a direct route to his destination.

Thou shalt prepare thee a way, and divide the coasts of thy land, which the Lord thy God giveth thee to inherit, into three parts, that every slayer may flee thither.

Deuteronomy 19:3

God wanted to make the way as easy as possible so He set up specific guidelines:

1. The path leading to the six cities of refuge had to be cleared of all obstacles.

2. The path was to be 50 to 60 feet wide.

3. The path was to be well marked at every turn with a sign that read, "This way to refuge city."

4. At the sign posts, an elder of the city was to point the way and encourage the person.

5. Every valley, river, and canyon must be bridged over, leading the person to safety and shelter.

What could the fleeing person expect once he arrived at the city of refuge? The book of Joshua provides the details:

The Lord also spake unto Joshua, saying, Speak to the children of Israel, saying, Appoint out for you cities of refuge, whereof I spake unto you by the hand of Moses: That the slayer that killeth any person unawares and unwittingly may flee thither: and they shall be your refuge from the avenger of blood. And when he that doth flee unto one of those cities shall stand at the entering of the gate of the city, and shall declare his cause in the ears of the elders of that city, they shall take him into the city unto them, and give him a place, that he may dwell among them. And if the avenger of blood pursue after him, then they shall not deliver the slayer up into his hand; because he smote his neighbour unwittingly, and hated him not beforetime. And he shall dwell in that city, until he stand before the congregation for judgment, and until the death of the high priest that shall be in those days: then shall the slayer return, and come unto his own city, and unto his own house, unto the city from whence he fled. Joshua 20:1-6

The elders of the cities of refuge were given certain responsibilities concerning the person seeking safety within their walls:

They were to hear what he had to say. As soon as the fleeing person arrived at the gates of the city, he was given the opportunity to tell his side of the story. The elders of the city were to listen to any victims fleeing for their lives.

This should be an example to us in the church. Before we condemn each other, we need to hear each other. Instead of accepting secondhand information, we need to get the facts from the person who made the mistake.

Next, the elders were to deliver the fleeing person—to snatch him out of the hands of the pursuing avenger. The people of the city provided protection, shielding him from those seeking to take his life in revenge.

Finally, the elders of the congregation were to restore the mistake-ridden victim. He was taken into the city as one of them and given a place to stay. The victim was totally accepted without reservation or condemnation.

To restore means, "to take back to its original form." We must restore broken marriages, fidelity and morality. While we do not condone the wrong, we do offer love, respect, and support. We all make mistakes and should be able to relate to others who find themselves in need of refuge.

The Shepherd's "Staff"

As I sat one evening outside my motel in Jerusalem, I witnessed something that altered my life forever.

An old shepherd was attempting to gather his flock into the fold before dark. A certain sense of urgency showed on his face as he led his sheep through a rough and rugged terrain.

When the two-inch long thorns pierced his wrinkled and callused hands, he nearly collapsed from the throbbing pain. To steady himself, he reached for his staff.

The staff of a shepherd has notches on which is inscribed the date of every victory the shepherd has won. These serve as reminders to give the shepherd confidence in future battles.

A pastor should be able to lean on his staff the way the shepherd's staff steadies him in shaky situations.

Today the word, "staff," has a different connotation. The staff of a pastor–his fellow workers–is vital to his ministry. A pastor should be able to lean on his staff the way the shepherd's staff steadies him in shaky situations. He should be able to put his full weight on the staff without causing collapse.

A pastor's staff should help him prepare the way for the flock and be willing to bleed as he bleeds. Like the staff of the shepherd, the church staff should have their pastor's victories engraved in their hearts so they can build him up in times of discouragement.

As I continued to watch the Jerusalem shepherd and his flock, I noticed that the goats had wandered off to feed at the garbage dump. I watched for the shepherd's response. He leaned on his staff and dropped his head in disgust.

As he went to retrieve them, the goats butted and kicked him and added insult to his injury. The only thing this shepherd had to lean on was his staff, which was tainted with his blood from the thorns.

When a pastor is wounded, bleeding, and weary, he needs to be able to lean on his staff and say, "I am a bleeding shepherd, a storm victim in need of a refuge. Can I lean on you? You are my staff, don't break. Don't let me fall!"

Your Blood Brothers

"Victims are on the run, fleeing for their lives as disaster hits the area! Lives have been lost, and many people are not accounted for. The hospitals are running over. The scene of the tragedy is a bloody mess. All races and people from every walk of life have been affected. The immediate need of the storm victims is refuge."

This could be the front page story of any newspaper after a tragic earthquake or major catastrophe. The most immediate need in such an emergency is to give attention without any bias or racial preference.

When Shepherds Bleed

In an emergency, no one takes time to place blame or point fingers. All that matters is that the needs of the victims are met.

In a natural disaster, the place of refuge must be well-marked. It must provide water, food, clothing, and warmth. Most of all, no matter what a person has done or become a victim of, he is to be received. A refuge center has to be diverse and balanced in meeting the needs of all those it protects.

Your ministry may have been shaken. The walls may be collapsing all around you. Everything is out of order and out of place, but you are still alive.

Maybe you are experiencing a marriage crisis, a mental crisis of depression, or spiritual burnout. You don't need someone to tell you your mistakes–you are a storm victim in need of refuge. You need to know where you can turn.

My prayer is that you will find that place of refuge in the midst of your storm. Whatever it is that is causing you to bleed, I pray that it will also cause you to cry out. Your cry will bring down a response from heaven.

Today there is a great demand for strong, definitive leadership in a way that has never been known in the history of the church. God has invested a great deal into your ministry, and now He wants to use the strength of other ministries to provide a place of refuge for you–a place where your dreams can be restored.

Your brothers and sisters in Christ are in covenant with you. In keeping with the Jewish covenant, we have cut our wrists to share in your bleeding. We are all of one blood–the blood of Jesus. That makes us blood brothers.

When shepherds bleed, may we be willing to give healing to–and receive healing from–our brothers.

We are all of one blood—
the blood of Jesus.
That makes us blood brothers.

uestions

1. List four ways in which the shepherd of the field is similar to the pastor of a church._____

_____

_____

_____

2. What areas of your life need to be replenished?_____

_____

_____

_____

3. Why is it important to cry out when you are overwhelmed?_____

_____

_____

_____

_____

4. Why did David feel that "refuge" had failed him? Have you ever felt that way? If so, explain._____

_____

_____

_____

5. Who and what makes Satan flee?_____

_____

_____

_____

6. Explain the three things that give us power over Satan._____

_____

_____

_____

7. Relate where you are in your Christian walk to Israel's journey through the desert._____

_____

_____

_____

8. What three classes of people were the cities of refuge set up to help?_____

_____

_____

_____

9. Provide a spiritual application for each of the five ways in which God made it easy for the fleeing person to find a city of refuge._____

_____

_____

_____

10. Name the three responsibilities of the elders of the cities of refuge._____

_____

_____

_____

11. List three ways in which a pastor's staff should function like a shepherd's staff._____

_____

_____

_____

12. When a fellow shepherd bleeds, explain what you can do to help._____

_____

_____

_____

13. Name your closest blood brothers in Christ and describe your commitment to them._____

_____

_____

_____

Notes

Notes

Notes

Printed in the United States
2277